All you need to know about the Maldives

Copyright © 2023 Jonas Hoffmann-Schmidt.
Translation: Linda Amber Chambers.

All rights reserved. This book, including all its parts, is protected by copyright. Any use outside the narrow limits of copyright law is prohibited without the written consent of the author. This book has been created using artificial intelligence to provide unique and informative content.

Disclaimer: This book is for entertainment purposes only. The information, facts and views contained therein have been researched and compiled to the best of our knowledge and belief. Nevertheless, the author and the publisher assume no liability for the accuracy or completeness of the information. Readers should consult with professionals before making any decisions based on this information. Use of this book is the responsibility of the reader.

Introduction: The fascination of the Maldives 6

Islands in the Indian Ocean: Geography of the Maldives 8

Underwater Paradise: The Coral Reefs of the Maldives 11

The Formation of the Maldives: Geological History 14

Early Settlement: The First Humans in the Maldives 16

Trade and Culture: The Historical Significance of the Maldives 18

Colonial Times: Maldivian History under Foreign Rule 21

Independence and Modernization: Developments in the 20th Century. 23

Maldivian Culture: Traditions and Customs 26

Religion in the Maldives: Islamic Influences 29

Dhivehi: The language of the Maldives 32

Island Lifestyle: The Everyday Life of the Locals 35

Dhoni and Fishing: The Maritime Culture of the Maldives 38

Culinary delights: The diversity of Maldivian cuisine 41

Exotic Flavors: Spices and Ingredients of the Maldives 44

Wildlife Encounters: Land and Sea Life 47

Endangered biodiversity: conservation in the Maldives 50

The underwater world: diving and snorkeling in clear waters 53

Male: capital and cultural center 56

The History of Malé: Glimpses of the Past 59

Malé today: Urban life in the capital 62

Addu City: Culture and History of the Second Largest Atoll 65

From Gan to Hulhulé: Cities Through the Ages 68

Fuvahmulah: The unique island of the Maldives 70

Traditional handicrafts: handicrafts of the locals 73

Festivals and celebrations: cultural highlights throughout the year 76

Architecture of the Maldives: Traditional construction methods and modern trends 79

Bodu Beru: Maldivian Music and Dance 82

Trade and Souvenirs: Shopping in the Maldives 84

History of Tourism: The Evolution of Tourism 87

Paradisiacal Resorts: Luxury Accommodations in the Maldives 90

Dreamy beaches and crystal clear waters: the attractions of the islands 93

Water Sports Paradise: Activities for the Adventurous 96

Maldivian Art Scene: Modern Artists and Their Works 99

Environmental Protection and Sustainability: The Maldives' Efforts 101

Travel Tips: Practical Information for Visiting the Maldives 104

Dive into History: Archaeological Sites and Wrecks 107

Maldivian Literature: Writers and Their Works 109

Clash of Cultures: Maldives and the Influence of Tourism 111

Looking to the Future: The Challenges and Opportunities for the Maldives 113

Epilogue 116

Introduction: The fascination of the Maldives

The glittering Indian Ocean is a paradise that enchants the senses and captures the imagination – the Maldives. This archipelago of 26 stunning atolls, consisting of over 1,000 coral islands, is undoubtedly one of the most fascinating destinations in the world. With its pristine beaches of dazzling white sand, turquoise waters and heady variety of marine life, the Maldives reveals a unique beauty that surpasses even the wildest dreams.

The magic of the Maldives begins with its geographical uniqueness. Spread over 90,000 square kilometers in the Indian Ocean, the islands are arranged in a way that will make any nature lover's heart beat faster. Each atoll is surrounded by vibrant coral reefs that are a mecca for divers and snorkelers. These reefs are home to an astonishing variety of marine life, from colorful fish to majestic sea turtles.

But the fascination of the Maldives does not end at the coasts. The underwater world is a microcosm of life, where more than 2,000 species of fish cavort and the reefs shine in a riot of colour. From tiny anemonefish that linger in the tentacles of their protective hosts to majestic whale sharks gliding gently through the waters, this maritime wonderland offers an unparalleled way to explore the beauty and complexity of the ocean.

However, the Maldives is more than just an aesthetic experience. Its rich history dates back centuries and reflects the influence of different cultures that have shaped the islands. From the first settlers who arrived here long ago, to the time of colonial rule and finally independence, every corner of the Maldives tells a story of resistance, adaptation and renewal. This historical depth gives the Maldives a soul that goes beyond the surface, creating a deep connection between the people and their land.

While the Maldives is known for its stunning natural beauty, it's also the local culture that makes these islands an unforgettable destination. The traditions, customs, and art forms of the locals reflect the rich history and religious beliefs that form the basis of their identity. From traditional dhivehi singing to intricately crafted crafts, the Maldives is a treasure trove of cultural diversity waiting to be discovered.

Islands in the Indian Ocean: Geography of the Maldives

The Maldives, a tropical island paradise in the Indian Ocean, fascinates not only with its natural beauty, but also with its unique geographical makeup. This archipelago covers an impressive area of about 90,000 square kilometers and is made up of 26 atolls, which in total include more than 1,000 coral islands. The geographical location of the Maldives, southwest of India and Sri Lanka, gives this region its distinctive features and makes it a sought-after destination for people from all over the world.

Each atoll of the Maldives is a ring of islands that stretches around a central lagoon. These atolls, in turn, are divided into smaller islands surrounded by stunning coral reefs. The formation of the atolls and islands is the result of a long geological history in which coral reefs have developed over millions of years. These reefs not only serve as a shelter for the islands from the waves of the ocean, but also as a natural breeding ground for an incredible variety of marine life.

The Maldives is known for its flat coral islands with rolling hills and palm trees rising above the azure waters. The average height of the islands is only 1.5 meters above sea level, which makes them extremely vulnerable to the effects of climate change and rising sea levels. This unique geographical feature has led locals to develop innovative technologies and approaches to coastal protection to protect the islands and their inhabitants.

The geography of the Maldives is closely linked to the ocean, which shapes the lives and culture of the locals. The islands offer an abundance of sea-related activities, including diving, snorkeling, surfing, and deep-sea fishing. The warm waters of the Indian Ocean are home not only to an impressive variety of fish species, but also to sea turtles, dolphins, sharks and manta rays.

The climate of the Maldives is tropical, characterized by a rainy and a dry season. Temperatures fluctuate only slightly throughout the year, ranging from a pleasant 25 to 31 degrees Celsius. The months of November to March are considered the dry season, while the rainy season lasts from April to October. These changing seasons affect not only the weather, but also marine life and the availability of certain activities.

The geography of the Maldives is closely linked to the local culture and people's lives. Reliance on the oceans for food and income has spawned a maritime culture that is reflected in traditions such as boat building, fishing, and coconut harvesting. Over the centuries, the locals have learned to live in harmony with nature and to use their resources sustainably.

The unique geographical location, the formation of the atolls and islands, the maritime life and the cultural connection with nature make the geography of the Maldives an indispensable part of the identity of this extraordinary archipelago.

Underwater Paradise: The Coral Reefs of the Maldives

The coral reefs of the Maldives are a unique oasis of life and beauty that captivates divers, snorkelers and sea lovers from all over the world. These reefs are not only a vibrant backdrop for dreamy holiday photos, but also an extremely important habitat for an incredible variety of marine life. The Maldives prides itself on being home to some of the best-preserved reefs in the world, and these reefs play a crucial role in the Indian Ocean ecosystem.

The coral reefs of the Maldives stretch for hundreds of kilometers along the coasts of the atolls. These reefs are the result of thousands of years of processes in which tiny coral polyps deposit their calcareous skeletons, building massive structures over time. These reefs form a maze of colorful gardens, impressive overhangs, narrow passageways, and mesmerizing underwater landscapes.

The biodiversity in the Maldivian coral reefs is breathtaking. Countless species of fish can be found here, from tiny anemonefish to majestic manta rays and playful dolphins. The coral reefs are also home to sea turtles, moray eels, barracuda, reef sharks, and more. The diversity of marine life is a feast for the eyes and attracts underwater photographers and nature lovers alike.

But the Maldives also faces challenges that threaten the health of its coral reefs. Coral bleaching, caused by rising water temperatures and environmental pressures, is one of the biggest threats to these fragile ecosystems. The Government of the Maldives and various environmental organizations are working to develop and implement measures to conserve and restore the reefs.

Snorkeling and diving in the coral reefs of the Maldives offers not only the opportunity to discover exotic marine life, but also the chance to experience the unique beauty and diversity of this underwater world up close. For beginners and experienced divers alike, there is an abundance of dive sites ranging from shallow reefs to deep drop-offs. These dives reveal a colorful world of corals, sponges, fish, and unexpected encounters.

The Maldivian coral reefs are also an important part of the local economy, as they power much of the tourism sector. Dive resorts and diving schools offer travelers the opportunity to explore the reefs and experience the unique adventure of underwater life. At the same time, it is of paramount importance to sustainably manage and protect the reefs in order to preserve their beauty and value for generations to come.

The coral reefs of the Maldives are more than just amazing sights – they are a living example of the wonders of nature and the fragile beauty of our planet. By understanding, protecting, and appreciating their importance, we can help preserve this underwater paradise for the future, while creating unforgettable experiences for travelers from all over the world. Welcome to the magical world of the Maldivian coral reefs.

The Formation of the Maldives: Geological History

The geological history of the Maldives is a fascinating chapter written over millions of years. This stunning chain of islands in the Indian Ocean is the result of a complex sequence of geological processes that have shaped the shape and structure of the atolls and islands.

The basis of the Maldives is an underwater mountain range known as the Chagos Laccadive Plateau. About 60 to 80 million years ago, volcanic activity began to form this plateau as magma erupted from the Earth's interior and accumulated layer by layer over time. The cooling lava formed basalt rocks and contributed to the formation of the underwater mountains, which eventually formed the basis for today's Maldives.

As the Chagos-Laccadive Plateau formed, the tectonic plates of the Earth's crust moved over long periods of time. The processes of plate tectonics caused the plateau to gradually rise above the ocean floor and eventually manifest itself in the current location of the Maldives. During the ascent, erosion helped shape and shape the surface of the plateau.

About 20 million years ago, volcanic activity began to decrease, and the plateau began to subside. The coral reefs that began to grow during this period moved into the emerging lagoons of the atolls, forming the characteristic reef structures that are so typical of the Maldives today. These reefs are made up of the calcareous skeletons of coral polyps, which accumulated over time and built up the reef structure.

During the last ice age, about 18,000 years ago, sea levels were significantly lower than they are today. The Maldives was part of the continental shelf that surrounded the region at the time. With the end of the Ice Age, glaciers began to melt, leading to a rise in sea levels. The rising water masses flooded the land areas and formed today's atolls, which were formed as a unique combination of reefs and islands.

The geological history of the Maldives is marked by an impressive sequence of events over millions of years. From volcanic activity and plate tectonics to the formation of coral reefs and the formation of today's islands, these processes are a reflection of the dynamic nature of our planet. The creation of the Maldives is a testament to how the forces of nature have shaped the country and how the inhabitants of these islands live and thrive in harmony with the circumstances.

Early Settlement: The First Humans in the Maldives

The early settlement history of the Maldives is a fascinating puzzle that gives us a glimpse into the beginnings of human presence on these remote islands. While it's hard to pinpoint exact dates, archaeological finds and historical records suggest that settlement in the Maldives began thousands of years ago.

It is believed that the first people to come to the Maldives were seafarers and fishermen who landed on the islands from the neighboring coasts of India, Sri Lanka and other surrounding areas. These early settlers were forced to adapt to the special conditions of the archipelago and adapt their lives to the resources of the sea. Coconut palms, fishing and maritime skills were vital to their survival.

The exact origin and identity of these first inhabitants remain partly obscure, as written records did not begin until much later. Nevertheless, there is evidence that the Maldives has been inhabited for at least 2,000 years. Archaeological finds of pottery, tools, and other artifacts on various islands suggest that these settlers developed a rudimentary culture and were able to settle on the islands.

Maldivian culture and society developed over the centuries under the influence of various cultures that came into contact with the Indian Ocean trade routes. Arab traders and seafarers played an important role in the introduction of Islam to the islands, which had a strong influence on the way of life and customs of the inhabitants.

The early settlement history of the Maldives is marked by oral traditions and legends that have been passed down from generation to generation. These stories tell of brave seafarers who landed on the islands, of the challenges of living on the remote islands, and of the emergence of local culture and identity. Although many of these stories have faded over time, they have nevertheless helped to preserve awareness of the roots of Maldivian society.

The first people in the Maldives may have left few traces, but their presence and heritage can still be felt today in the traditions, customs and everyday life of the locals. The beginnings of settlement are a testament to the human ability to adapt to diverse environments and to the close connection between people and their land.

Trade and Culture: The Historical Significance of the Maldives

Nestled in the sparkling Indian Ocean, the Maldives has played a remarkable role throughout history as major trading hubs and cultural crossroads. The geographical location of this archipelago between India and Arabia gave the Maldives a strategic position that allowed traders from all over the world to cross these waters and trade. This historical significance not only shaped the economic development of the Maldives, but also left behind a rich cultural diversity that can still be felt today.

Centuries ago, the Maldives established itself as a hub on the ancient trade routes that connected the East and the West. Arabian sailors who sailed through the Indian Ocean on their dhoni made the Maldives an important port of call. The trade in goods such as spices, precious stones, pearls, sandalwood, and exotic goods flourished in the markets of the Maldives.

The Maldives also became an important center of Islamic trade and played a crucial role in the spread of Islam in the region. Arab traders brought not only goods but also their religion and culture to the islands. Islam became an integral part of life in the Maldives over the centuries, and the islanders adopted the religious practices and customs of Arab sailors.

During the heyday of the Silk Road, which connected the Orient with Europe, the Maldives experienced a brisk trade in exotic goods from Asia and Africa. These trade routes brought wealth, knowledge and cultural exchange to the islands. The local population benefited from the variety of goods traded in the markets, and the islands became a melting pot of cultures.

The historical importance of the Maldives as a commercial hub is also reflected in the architecture, art forms and traditions of the islanders. Arabic influences are visible in the designs of mosques, in the clothing and in the language of the Maldives. Even the traditional boat-building art of the Dhonis was shaped by contact with foreign seafarers.

Maldivian culture is thus a living testimony to the historical connections and cultural exchanges made possible by trade. The diversity of influences has helped to create a unique identity that combines elements from the Orient, Africa and Asia. This cultural heritage is still cherished and nurtured today, and locals pride themselves on keeping alive the memories of the Maldives' historical significance as a trading hub.

The history of trade and culture in the Maldives is a fascinating journey through time, showing us the close connection between people, their activities and their environment.

Colonial Times: Maldivian History under Foreign Rule

Maldivian history under foreign rule is a captivating chapter that directed the movements of world history to the distant shores of these islands in the Indian Ocean. The Maldives, which occupied a strategic position due to its geographical location between India and Arabia, became over the centuries the plaything of the colonial powers and political interests that influenced and shaped the fate of the islands.

The colonial period for the Maldives began in the 16th century when the Portuguese set their eyes on these islands. They came with the aim of trading and expanding their power. However, the locals stubbornly resisted the Portuguese conquest and were able to liberate the islands after some time. However, the period under Portuguese rule left its mark, especially in the form of Christianity, which was briefly introduced.

In the 17th century, the Dutch came to the waters of the Maldives and also tried to exert influence on the islands. They presented themselves as allies of the local rulers, but managed to establish trade monopolies and wield political power. However, after a period of time, the Dutch lost their interest in the Maldives and withdrew. The 19th century brought the British East India Company onto the scene. The Maldives fell under the shadow of British imperialism when it became a protectorate of the British Empire. Although the locals retained a certain autonomy, the British had influence on the political and economic development of the islands. The British presence also left a trail of modernization as infrastructure and education were promoted on the islands.

The colonial era of the Maldives did not end until 1965, when the islands gained their independence from Great Britain. However, this independence did not come without compromise, as the Maldives had previously signed a treaty that gave the British control over certain defense and foreign policy issues. In 1968, the Maldives was declared a republic, and Ibrahim Nasir became the first president of the independent country. Maldivian history under foreign rule is a complex of political shifts, cultural influences, and economic changes. The traces of the Portuguese, Dutch and British presence can still be felt today in various aspects of Maldivian life. This period has also highlighted the resilience and adaptability of the locals, who have preserved their identity and culture despite the changing dominions.

Independence and Modernization: Developments in the 20th Century.

The 20th century brought profound changes to the Maldives, ushering the country into a new era of independence and modernization. After centuries of foreign rule and colonial influences, the Maldives began to shape its own identity and face the challenges and opportunities of the modern world.

The independence of the Maldives was recognized by Great Britain in 1965, after the islands had previously been under the shadow of the British Empire. Independence marked the beginning of a phase for the Maldives of building its own national identity and shaping an independent foreign policy. Ibrahim Nasir was elected as the first president of the independent country and initiated reforms in various areas.

The development of infrastructure and education were central elements of the modernization efforts. Roads, ports, airports, and communications facilities have been built to improve the islands' connectivity to the global network. Educational institutions have been modernized to meet the demands of a changing world, and the promotion of education has become a key goal of the government.

The Maldives also began to engage internationally by establishing diplomatic relations with other countries and becoming a member of international organizations. These moves helped the Maldives establish its presence on the global stage and represent the country's interests in the international arena. Participation in the international community opened up new opportunities for trade, cooperation and cultural exchange.

From an economic point of view, tourism has played a crucial role in the modernization of the Maldives. In the 1970s, the Maldives opened up to international tourism, attracting visitors with its stunning beaches, coral reefs, and picturesque islands. This move brought about an economic boom that diversified revenue streams and created new opportunities for jobs and growth.

However, developments in the 20th century also brought challenges. The changes in lifestyle and economy led to environmental impacts that endangered the fragile ecology of the Maldives. Rising sea levels and climate change threatened the existence of the low-lying islands, forcing the government to take measures to protect and adapt to climate change.

The Maldives went through political upheavals that shaped the nation. The transition from a republic to democracy in 2008 marked an important step towards political openness and participation. However, democratization also brought with it political uncertainties and tensions that challenged Maldivian society.

The 20th century was marked by a constant quest by the Maldives to modernize and adapt to a changing world. Developments in this century have shaped Maldivian society, leading it on a journey of transformation while preserving its unique identity and culture. The Maldives has evolved from a colonial past into an independent, modern state that is facing global challenges and opportunities.

Maldivian Culture: Traditions and Customs

Maldivian culture is a fascinating mosaic of traditions, customs and values that shape the identity of the islanders. This culture, which has been shaped over centuries, reflects people's unique connection with their environment and history. From the art and music to the social norms and religious practices, the traditions of the Maldives have a deep meaning in the daily lives of the locals.

Religion plays a central role in Maldivian culture. Islam, which was brought to the islands in the 12th century, is the cornerstone of life and shapes people's customs, way of life and moral values. Maldivian society is steeped in Islamic traditions, from the daily prayer times to the celebrations during Ramadan.

An important aspect of Maldivian culture is the close connection between people and the sea. The sea is not only an important source of food and economy, but also an integral part of the lifestyle of the locals. Fishing and maritime activities are deeply rooted in Maldivian identity, and the traditions of boatbuilding and fishing are passed down from generation to generation.

The arts and crafts of the Maldives are an expression of the creative skills of the locals. Handmade products such as mats, baskets, carvings and traditional musical instruments show the attention to detail and care that goes into the artistic design. The traditional music, accompanied by drums and flutes, is an important part of the cultural events and celebrations on the islands.

Festivals and celebrations are an opportunity for people to celebrate their community and culture. The most important festival in the Maldives is Eid al-Fitr, which marks the end of Ramadan. During this time, families and friends come together to pray, celebrate, and give gifts to each other. Another significant celebration is Independence Day on July 26, when the Maldives celebrates its sovereignty.

The traditional clothing of the Maldives reflects the cultural diversity and religious values. Men often wear the sarong, a long wrap dress, while women wear the libaas, a long dress with a headscarf. These garments are not only an expression of culture, but also practical for living in the warm climate conditions of the islands.

Maldivian culture has adapted to changing circumstances over time, but still retains its unique identity. The customs, traditions and values of the locals are a reflection of the close relationship with nature, religion and history. Maldivian culture is vibrant, diverse and proud, and it remains an important part of life on these fascinating islands in the Indian Ocean.

Religion in the Maldives: Islamic Influences

Religion in the Maldives is inextricably linked to Islam, which has played a dominant role in the lives of locals since the 12th century. Islam has profoundly influenced Maldivian culture, society, and customs, and is an integral part of daily life on these islands in the Indian Ocean.

The introduction of Islam to the Maldives dates back to Arab traders and sailors who traveled to the waters of the Indian Ocean over the centuries. The influences of these seafarers brought Islam to the Maldives and shaped the religious and cultural life of the islanders. The adoption of Islam led to a transformation of social structures, legislation and religious practices.

Islam is the state religion in the Maldives, and the constitution recognizes only Sunni Islam. The majority of locals are Sunni Muslims, and the religious rites and customs are an integral part of daily life. The five daily prayers, fasting during Ramadan, pilgrimage to Mecca (Hajj) and charity (Zakat) are important pillars of faith practiced by the locals.

The mosque is a central element of religious life in the Maldives. Locals regularly visit the mosques to pray and receive spiritual guidance. Friday prayers are especially important when the community comes together to pray together and listen to the Imam's sermon. The mosques serve not only as places of prayer, but also as centers for social interaction and education.

Maldivian culture and society are strongly influenced by Islamic values and norms. The clothing of the locals is conservative, with women often wearing the headscarf and men dressed in long sarongs. Alcohol is prohibited for locals in the Maldives, and compliance with Islamic laws and norms is a matter of course for residents.

The Maldivian government has been committed to preserving and promoting Islam as an integral part of the country. Religious educational institutions and programs are supported to deepen knowledge of Islam and strengthen religious identity. The religious calendar of the Maldives is marked by important Islamic holidays, including Eid al-Fitr, Eid al-Adha, and the birthday of the Prophet Muhammad.

Islamization has shaped Maldivian culture, creating a deep connection between religion, identity, and lifestyle. The locals value their religious upbringing and the values of Islam, which give them orientation in life. The Islamic influences are omnipresent and palpable in the traditions, customs and social interaction of the people of the Maldives.

Dhivehi: The language of the Maldives

The Dhivehi language, also known as Divehi or Maldivian Dhivehi, is the native language of the Maldives and an integral part of the Maldivian identity. Spoken by the locals on the islands in the Indian Ocean, it is a window into the rich culture and history of this island nation.

Dhivehi belongs to the Indo-Aryan language family and is closely related to Sinhala in Sri Lanka. It uses its own alphabet called Thaana, which consists of 24 letters written from right to left. Thaana differs significantly from the alphabet systems of the surrounding regions and contributes to the uniqueness of the language.

The origins of the Dhivehi language go back a long way into the history of the Maldives. It is believed that the language has been spoken on the islands for centuries and has evolved over time. Through contacts with various cultures and trading partners in the Indian Ocean, Arabic, Persian and South Indian influences have also crept into the language over time.

The Dhivehi language has a rich literary tradition dating back to the 12th century. Writers and poets have written poems, stories, and religious works in Dhivehi. Especially during the Islamic era of the Maldives, many religious texts were written in Dhivehi to spread the beliefs and teachings of Islam.

The language has changed and adapted over time to meet the needs of society. Modern Dhivehi words often have influences from English, Arabic, and other languages due to trade, tourism, and global communication. However, despite these changes, Dhivehi remains a central element of the cultural identity of the Maldives.

The language plays a crucial role in Maldivian society as it serves as a means of communication, education and cultural transmission. It is present in schools and educational institutions and is passed on from generation to generation. The language connects the people on the islands and contributes to strengthening national cohesion.

The preservation and promotion of the Dhivehi language is a concern of the Maldivian government and community. There are efforts to preserve the language in all areas of life, whether in educational institutions, in the media, or in cultural events. The recognition and cultivation of the language is of great importance in order to preserve the cultural diversity and identity of the Maldives.

Dhivehi is more than just a form of communication; it is a living testament to the history, culture and people of the Maldives. It connects the past with the present and helps to preserve the unique identity of the islanders. The Dhivehi language remains a symbol of Maldivian culture and an expression of the diversity and resilience of this fascinating island nation.

Island Lifestyle: The Everyday Life of the Locals

The island lifestyle in the Maldives is characterized by a unique connection between the people and their environment. The daily life of the locals on these remote islands in the Indian Ocean reflects the peculiarities of Maldivian culture, religion and geography. From fishing to family community, from traditional crafts to modern developments, the island lifestyle is a kaleidoscope of Maldivian life.

The rhythm of life in the Maldives is closely linked to the tides and the sea. Fishing is not only an important economic activity, but also an integral part of the lives of the locals. Early in the morning, the fishermen deploy their dhonis, traditional boats, into the clear waters of the ocean and return after a long day with a rich catch. Fish is not only a main source of food, but also a symbol of community cohesion.

The community plays a significant role in the daily life of the locals. Social ties are strong, and families are at the heart of Maldivian society. The traditional Maldivian community structure, known as "Hakuraa", encourages cooperation, solidarity and support among the locals. Joint activities, festivals and celebrations strengthen bonds between people and help maintain community values.

The architecture of Maldivian houses reflects adaptation to climatic conditions. The traditional "Ganduvaru" houses are built of coral stone and palm leaves and have been designed to provide natural ventilation and cooling. In modern times, the architecture on the islands has evolved to meet the needs of the rising population, while preserving the Maldivian identity features.

The traditions and customs of the locals are present in many aspects of everyday life. The clothing, music, food and celebrations are infused with the rich Maldivian culture. Traditional clothing, such as the sarong for men and the libaas for women, is ubiquitous in society. Traditional musical instruments such as the "Bodu Beru" - a kind of drum - accompany the festivities and events.

The importance of Islam in the daily life of the locals cannot be overemphasized. The five daily prayers, fasting during Ramadan and the observance of religious laws shape people's daily routines. The mosques are not only places of prayer, but also centers of community where locals come together to pray, learn and engage in social interaction.

In recent decades, technological advances and tourism have transformed Maldivian society. Modern conveniences, communication technologies, and educational opportunities have made their way in, expanding the lifestyle of the locals. At the same time, efforts are underway to preserve traditional values and customs and integrate them into modern life.

The island lifestyle of the locals is a harmonious interplay of tradition and modernity. The people of the Maldives are preserving their identity as they face the challenges of the changing world. From fishing to family, from traditional homes to modern amenities, the island lifestyle is a fascinating portrait of the Maldivian way of life and culture.

Dhoni and Fishing: The Maritime Culture of the Maldives

The maritime culture of the Maldives is deeply rooted in the history and everyday life of the locals. The dhoni, a traditional boat, and fishing are central elements of this culture and reflect people's close relationship with the waters of the Indian Ocean. Passed down from generation to generation, dhoni and fishing are not only economic activities, but also a symbol of the Maldives' identity and lifestyle.

The dhoni, once made of wood, are a characteristic feature of Maldivian shipping. These handcrafted boats are used for various purposes, but mainly for fishing. The construction of the dhoni is adapted to the conditions of the ocean – its shallow shape allows it to easily navigate shallow waters, while its sturdy hulls make it seaworthy. The dhoni are a living example of the craftsmanship of the locals and their ability to adapt to the natural conditions.

Fishing is one of the oldest and most important economic activities in the Maldives. The locals have always depended on the rich fishing grounds of the Indian Ocean, which are home to a rich variety of marine life. Fishing is not only a source of income, but also an integral part of Maldivian diet and culture. Fish such as tuna, mackerel and barracuda are main ingredients of Maldivian cuisine.

Fishing in the Maldives comes in a variety of forms, from traditional hand-line fishing to the more modern technique of trawling. Handline fishing is a traditional method in which fishermen fish with handmade hooks. This method is more sustainable and less harmful to the marine environment compared to modern techniques. However, fishing also has challenges, including overfishing and environmental impacts.

The maritime culture of the Maldives spans different aspects of life. In addition to fishing, boats play an important role in transport, trade and tourism. The dhoni are not only used for fishing, but also for transporting people and goods between the islands. They are an essential part of island life and shape the image of the Maldivian coasts.

Maritime culture also has a social dimension. Fishermen often work together in close-knit communities, sharing their knowledge of the oceans, tides, and fishing techniques. Dhoni fishing is not only an economic activity, but also a social event where communities come together to share the day's catches and share stories.

Dhoni and fishing are inextricably linked to the identity of the Maldives. They reflect the locals' adaptability, skills, and relationship with the natural environment. Maritime culture is a vibrant expression of the Maldivian lifestyle, closely linked to the waters of the Indian Ocean.

Culinary delights: The diversity of Maldivian cuisine

Maldivian cuisine is a true delight for the senses and a reflection of the diverse cultures and influences that have come together on the islands of the Indian Ocean over the centuries. With an abundance of fresh seafood, exotic spices and local ingredients, Maldivian cuisine offers a unique dining experience that immerses guests in the rich culture of the islands.

Seafood is at the heart of Maldivian cuisine. Fish, tuna, and seafood are plentiful and prepared in a variety of ways. A well-known dish is "Mas Huni", a salad made with minced tuna, coconut and spices, which is often served for breakfast. Another popular dish is "Rihaakuru", a type of fish sauce that is often used as a condiment for many dishes.

Rice is a staple in the Maldivian diet and forms the basis of many dishes. "Garudiya" is a fish soup with rice, which is prepared with coconut milk and spices and is regularly served in many households. Rice is also often served with curry dishes such as "hedhikaa" (fried pastries) or "rihaakuru".

Maldivian cuisine is characterized by its use of fresh spices and herbs, which add flavor and aroma to the dishes. Commonly used spices include cardamom, cinnamon, turmeric, ginger, and chilies. Not only do these spices add a unique flavor to dishes, but they are also part of the cultural identity of Maldivian cuisine.

Coconut is another central element in the Maldivian diet. Coconut milk, coconut oil, and grated coconut are used in many dishes to give them creaminess and flavor. "Kiru Kiru" is a popular snack that involves mixing grated coconut with sugar and spices.

Traditional desserts are also a delight in Maldivian cuisine. "Bajiya" are deep-fried dumplings filled with coconut and sugar, often served on special occasions or celebrations. "Foni Boakiba" is a sweet pastry made from rice, coconut and sugar fried in coconut oil.

Maldivian cuisine is not only a culinary experience, but also a reflection of the culture and way of life of the locals. Traditionally, meals are often taken sitting on the floor, with family and friends coming together to enjoy the delicious food. The culinary traditions and customs are an important part of the Maldivian identity and community.

With the advent of tourism, modern influences have also crept into Maldivian cuisine. The resorts and hotels offer international dishes to cater to the different tastes of guests. Nevertheless, traditional Maldivian cuisine remains an indispensable part of island life and a way to experience the unique culture and history of the Maldives.

Exotic Flavors: Spices and Ingredients of the Maldives

The spices and ingredients of the Maldives are a feast for the senses and a central part of the island nation's rich culinary traditions. The variety of exotic flavors reflects the historical influences, geographical location, and the locals' close connection to nature. From fresh seafood to aromatic spices, Maldivian ingredients bring flavour and colour to traditional dishes, immersing guests in the fascinating world of Maldivian cuisine.

The Maldives, surrounded by the clear waters of the Indian Ocean, is rich in fresh seafood. Tuna is undoubtedly one of the main ingredients in Maldivian cuisine and is prepared in a variety of ways. From "Mas Huni" (tuna salad) to "Rihaakuru" (fish sauce), all parts of the tuna are used to add flavor and texture to the dishes. In addition to tuna, mackerel, barracuda and crabs are also common ingredients.

The use of spices gives Maldivian dishes their characteristic flavor and depth. Spices such as cardamom, cinnamon, turmeric, ginger, and chilies are often used in various combinations to add a balance of spice and flavor to dishes. These spices are not only important for taste, but also have medicinal and health benefits that are appreciated by the locals.

Coconut is another key ingredient in Maldivian cuisine. From coconut milk to coconut oil, grated coconut to coconut sugar, it is used in various forms to add flavor and texture to dishes. Coconut is a natural source of fats, vitamins and minerals and contributes to the rich culinary palette of the Maldives.

Local harvesting and agriculture also play a role in the supply of fresh ingredients. Fruits such as bananas, papaya, mango and jackfruit are popular in Maldivian cuisine and are often used in desserts, juices and snacks. Agriculture also offers vegetables such as eggplant, okra and pumpkin, which find their place in various curry dishes.

Maldivian cuisine is also characterized by the use of native herbs and leaves. "Murry", a leaf used in many dishes, gives the food a distinctive taste and fragrance. It is often used in curries and stews. "Fehi", on the other hand, is a fragrant herb used in drinks and sweets to give dishes a fresh aroma.

The combination of these exotic ingredients gives Maldivian dishes a unique identity and a variety of flavors. Locals appreciate the local ingredients not only for their taste, but also for their cultural significance and historical connection to the Maldivian way of life. The exotic flavors brought forth by the spices, seafood, coconut, and other ingredients make Maldivian cuisine a culinary experience that invites guests to enjoy the authentic culture and tradition of the Maldives.

Wildlife Encounters: Land and Sea Life

The wildlife of the Maldives is as diverse and fascinating as the islands themselves. Both on land and in the turquoise sea, there is a rich variety of animal species that amaze visitors. From exotic birds and native reptiles to colorful fish and majestic sea creatures, the Maldives' wildlife offers an unforgettable encounter with nature.

The islands of the Maldives are home to a number of native animals that have adapted to life on the small landmasses. Among the native birds is the "Dhondheeni" or white-breasted flycatcher, which is native to the densely vegetated coastal regions. Also on display is the "koakoa", a characteristic rail bird that can be found in the swamps and mangrove areas.

The reptile world of the Maldives also includes some endemic species. The "Gurahali" or Maldivian geckos are common on the islands and can often be found in the homes of the locals. The native geckos play an important role in the ecosystem as they control insect populations and thus maintain balance in nature.

However, the true splendor of the Maldives' wildlife is revealed beneath the surface of the Indian Ocean. The coral reefs that surround the islands are a paradise for snorkelers and divers alike. Colorful corals of all shapes and sizes create a breathtaking underwater panorama. The reefs are home to a dazzling variety of fish species, from tiny anemonefish to majestic manta rays.

The Maldives is also known for its shark populations, including the majestic whale shark and the playful reef shark. These gentle giants of the sea attract divers from all over the world, who take the opportunity to get up close and personal with these impressive creatures. The sea turtles are also a symbol of Maldivian wildlife, as they nest and feed in the islands' protected waters.

The encounter with the wildlife of the Maldives goes beyond the boundaries of the water. During guided island tours and nature excursions, visitors often have the opportunity to observe native animals in their natural habitat. The nature reserves on the islands contribute to the conservation and protection of wildlife, allowing visitors to admire the unique species and learn more about efforts to protect the environment.

The wildlife of the Maldives is a living example of the beauty and diversity of nature. From the native birds and reptiles on the islands to the colourful schools of fish and majestic marine life in the reefs, the wildlife of the Maldives offers an unparalleled experience for nature lovers and adventurers. It is a testament to the amazing biodiversity of the islands and a reminder of how precious and worthy of protection our natural world is.

Endangered biodiversity: conservation in the Maldives

Conservation in the Maldives plays a prominent role as the island nation faces the challenges of climate change and environmental protection. The unique biodiversity of the Maldives is of great importance as the islands are home to many endemic and endangered species. From protecting coral reefs to preserving native wildlife, conservation efforts in the Maldives are vital to preserving the environment for future generations.

The coral reefs of the Maldives are one of the most biodiverse ecosystems in the world, but they are also extremely vulnerable to climate change and human activities. Rising ocean temperatures and ocean acidification are threatening coral bleaching, which can lead to coral death. To ensure the protection of coral reefs, the Maldives has established protected areas and taken measures to promote sustainable tourism and fishing.

The native animal species of the Maldives are also important for conservation. Sea turtles, including the green sea turtle and loggerhead sea turtle, nest on the beaches of the Maldives. These turtles are endangered and protected to preserve their reproduction and habitat. Populations of sharks and manta rays are also threatened by illegal fishing and marine pollution, and therefore conservation measures are being taken to protect these majestic animals.

Another important nature conservation project concerns the preservation of native plant life. The vegetation on the islands is adapted to the specific climatic conditions, and some plants are endemic. Mangrove forests play an important role in coastal protection and in supporting the marine life cycle. The Maldives is committed to the conservation and restoration of these important ecosystems.

The Maldives is also a prime example of the effects of rising sea levels as a result of climate change. The low-lying islands are particularly vulnerable to sea level rise, which threatens their coastlines and habitats. The Maldives is committed to climate protection internationally and is working to make its own activities more sustainable to counteract the negative effects of climate change.

The locals play a crucial role in the conservation of the Maldives. Community-based initiatives promote environmental education and awareness-raising in local communities. Sustainable tourism also plays a role in conservation, as resorts and hotels take measures to reduce the ecological footprint.

Conservation in the Maldives is a continuous process that preserves the uniqueness of the islands and their biodiversity. The threats of climate change and human activities require joint efforts at the global and local levels to preserve nature and the environment for generations to come. Conservation efforts are an important step in protecting the Maldives' rich biodiversity and securing the sustainable future of this stunning island nation.

The underwater world: diving and snorkeling in clear waters

The Maldives is known worldwide for its stunning marine life, which attracts divers and snorkelers from all over the world. The clear, turquoise waters, rich in biodiversity, offer a unique experience that amazes every visitor. From colorful coral reefs to majestic marine life, the underwater world of the Maldives offers an unforgettable adventure for nature lovers and adventurers.

The coral reefs of the Maldives are one of the main attractions for divers and snorkelers. The reefs stretch for hundreds of kilometers and offer a rich variety of coral species, including table corals, brain corals, fan corals, and many more. These corals form the basis of a complex ecosystem that is home to abundant marine life.

The Maldivian reefs are also home to an impressive variety of fish species. From tiny clownfish that live in the anemones to large schools of fish that roam the reefs, there's a dazzling array of marine life to discover here.

Some of the most popular species that delight divers and snorkelers include the colorful Napoleon wrasse, the playful parrotfish, and the elegant butterflyfish.

Encounters with large animals are also a highlight of the Maldivian underwater world. Whale sharks, the largest fish in the world, are native to the waters of the Maldives and can often be spotted on guided dives. Manta rays, with their impressive wings, glide majestically through the reefs, offering divers an unforgettable spectacle.

For snorkelers, the shallow waters of the lagoons offer an ideal opportunity to explore the underwater world. The clear waters allow an excellent view of the coral reefs and the colorful variety of fish. Snorkelers can admire the beauty of the reefs and marine life from the surface without having to dive deep.

The Maldives also offers unique underwater formations such as "Thilas" and "Giris". Thilas are underwater seamounts that rise from the depths and are home to an abundance of marine life. Giris, on the other hand, are small coral islands that rise from the depths and can be explored by snorkelers and divers. These geological features contribute to the diversity of underwater experiences in the Maldives.

Diving tourism is well developed in the Maldives, with many world-class dive resorts and diving schools suitable for beginners to experienced divers. Dive sites vary from shallow reefs to depths that appeal to experienced divers. Diving conditions are excellent all year round, with warm water temperatures and good visibility.

The underwater world of the Maldives is a treasure to be preserved. Sustainable tourism and the protection of coral reefs help preserve biodiversity and the beauty of the marine environment for future generations. Diving and snorkeling in the clear waters of the Maldives is one way to experience the fascinating underwater world and enjoy the beauty of nature in its purest form.

Male: capital and cultural center

The capital of the Maldives, Male, is more than just a geographical point on the map – it is the cultural, political and economic heart of the island nation. Located in the Indian Ocean, Male is a small but vibrant city that offers a rich history and a unique atmosphere. As a political hub, it houses government institutions, embassies and important institutions, while at the same time as a cultural hub it reflects the diversity of Maldivian arts, customs and lifestyles.

Male is one of the most densely populated capitals in the world and is characterized by an interesting mix of modern architecture and traditional Maldivian culture. The city covers an area of only about 2.2 square kilometers, making it a compact metropolis. However, despite its limited size, Male has an impressive number of things to see and do.

The historic Hukuru Miskiy Mosque, also known as the Friday Mosque, is one of the city's most impressive landmarks. With its carved coral columns and ornate woodwork, the mosque is an example of traditional

Maldives architecture. The adjacent Hukuru Miskiy Museum offers a glimpse into the island's religious and cultural history.

Another cultural highlight is Sultan's Park, which once housed the royal palace. Today, the park is home to the National Museum of the Maldives, which showcases a comprehensive collection of artifacts and exhibits from the country's history. Ranging from ancient sculptures to regal regalia, the exhibits offer visitors the chance to immerse themselves in the Maldives' rich past.

Male's vibrant markets, such as the fish market and vegetable market, are a reflection of the daily lives of the locals. Here, visitors can discover fresh seafood, spices, tropical fruits, and handmade souvenirs. The markets are a melting pot of activity and the perfect place to experience the local culture first-hand.

Male's skyline is dominated by modern buildings and skyscrapers that reflect the growth and development of the city. In recent decades, numerous luxury hotels, restaurants, shopping malls and cultural institutions have established themselves in the capital to meet the needs of locals and the growing number of tourists.

Despite the modern development, Male still retains its charm as a place where traditional customs and values are maintained. The locals are proud of their cultural identity and their hospitality. The streets of Male are lined with colourful houses, small shops and restaurants serving local specialties.

Male is also home to many cultural events and festivals that celebrate the rich culture of the Maldives. The Kuda Eid Festival and the Independence Festival are just two examples of the city's vibrant festival culture, where locals and visitors come together to enjoy music, dance, and traditions.

The capital, Male, is thus not only an administrative centre, but also a cultural centre that reflects the history, arts and daily life of the Maldives. With a mix of historical significance, modern development and cultural richness, Male is a fascinating place that offers an insight into the diversity and dynamism of Maldivian society.

The History of Malé: Glimpses of the Past

The city of Malé, capital of the Maldives, is not only a modern center of activity, but also a place with a rich and fascinating history. The origins of Malé go far back in time and reflect the development and transformation of the Maldives over the centuries. The city's history is marked by trade, culture, colonial influence and the preservation of Maldivian identity.

While the exact origin of Malé is not accurately dated in history, it is believed that settlement of the island began several centuries ago. The local population lived in simple settlements and made a living from fishing and trade with surrounding regions. Malé developed into an important trading center in the Indian Ocean, as the island's strategic location allowed the trade in spices, precious stones, pearls, and other goods.

Over the centuries, Malé experienced various outside influences, including Arab traders, Portuguese explorers, and Dutch colonial powers. These influences have shaped the culture, architecture and customs of the city.

During Portuguese rule in the 16th century, Malé became a center for Islam and local culture, which is still visible today in the architecture of the mosques and historic buildings.

In the 17th century, the Dutch took control of the Maldives and introduced the islands into the colonial era. The Maldives paid tribute to the colonial rulers, who in turn supported the local ruling dynasty. This period of foreign rule left its mark on the history of the Maldives and shaped the country's relationship with the outside world.

With British colonization in the 19th century, the Maldives became a protectorate of the British Empire. During this period, Malé remained the political and cultural center of the country. The inhabitants of Malé maintained their identity and traditions despite the colonial influences. In 1965, the Maldives gained its independence from Great Britain, and Malé became the capital of the newly formed republic.

The history of Malé reflects not only the political changes, but also the resilience and adaptability of the locals. The city has evolved from a small settlement to a modern urban centre that preserves the cultural diversity and native identity of the Maldives. Malé's historical sites, monuments, and museums offer visitors insight into the country's rich history and its evolution over time.

The history of Malé is one of change, adaptation and preservation. From its humble beginnings as a commercial hub to the current capital of the Maldives, Malé reflects the development and spirit of the island nation. The city's history is an important part of the Maldives' cultural heritage and a window into the past that lays the foundation for the country's present and future.

Malé today: Urban life in the capital

Malé, the vibrant capital of the Maldives, is now an exciting hub of urban life, offering an intriguing blend of tradition and modernity. With a population of around 150,000 people, the city is the political, economic and cultural heart of the island nation. Malé is not only a place where government institutions and businesses are located, but also a vibrant community of locals that reflects the diversity of Maldivian culture.

Malé's skyline is dominated by modern buildings, skyscrapers and skyscrapers that symbolize the city's development as an economic center. Banks, shops, hotels and restaurants stretch along the waterfront, offering a variety of services for locals and tourists alike. The modern cityscape contrasts with the traditional architecture that has been preserved in the narrow streets and alleys of the city.

The residents of Malé are a diverse community made up of people from different ethnic backgrounds, religions, and lifestyles. This diversity is reflected in the city's cultural scene, which offers a wide range of artistic expressions, music, dance and theatre. Art galleries, cultural centers, and event venues are a venue for creative activities and the exchange of ideas.

Urban life in Malé is hectic and energetic, with the streets teeming with activity, be it the busy traffic, markets or bustling cafes. People rush to work, do their shopping, meet up with friends and enjoy the city's diverse gastronomic offer. The local cuisine, which is characterized by fresh seafood, tropical fruits and spices, can be enjoyed on street corners and in restaurants alike.

Despite the urban lifestyle, the inhabitants of Malé still preserve their cultural customs and traditions. Islam plays a central role in the city's daily life, from the chants from the mosques to the religious celebrations and festivals Close community building and mutual support are an important part of Malé's social fabric.

Education is highly valued in Malé, and the city is home to some of the best educational institutions in the country. Universities, schools and research institutions offer residents the opportunity to further their academic education and specialize in various disciplines.

However, the challenges of urban life in Malé are also palpable. The limited space of the city, the increasing population and the environmental impact of urban growth are issues that influence urban planning and quality of life. The government and the city administration are working to find sustainable solutions to these challenges and to make urban life in Malé livable and sustainable.

Overall, Malé is now a vibrant, diverse and exciting urban hub that reflects the dynamism and facets of Maldivian society. Synonymous with progress, cultural identity and community spirit, the city offers visitors and residents alike the opportunity to experience the fascinating world of the Maldives from an urban perspective.

Addu City: Culture and History of the Second Largest Atoll

Addu City, also known as Addu Atoll, is the second largest atoll in the Maldives and a place of great cultural and historical significance. Located in the south of the island nation, the atoll covers an area of about 153 square kilometers and consists of numerous islands and lagoons characterized by impressive natural beauty. The history and culture of Addu City reflect the diversity of Maldivian society and tell of a rich past that is closely linked to the atoll's trade, politics and communities.

The origins of Addu City go back a long way into the history of the Maldives. The inhabitants of the atoll once lived from agriculture, fishing and trade. The geographical location of Addu City, close to the important sea route between India and the Maldives, made it a significant stopover for merchant ships and seafarers. This trade not only brought prosperity but also led to cultural exchange processes and influenced the way of life of the inhabitants of Addu City.

During the colonial period, Addu City played an important role in the political landscape of the Maldives. During British colonization, the atoll served as a strategic base for the British Navy and was the scene of important political events. The British military base in Addu City was also an important factor in relations between the Maldives and Great Britain.

Addu City is also known for its rich culture and traditions. The inhabitants of the atoll cultivate their cultural identity through music, dance, handicrafts and customs. Addu City's local cuisine reflects the variety of seafood and agricultural produce available in the region. Traditional festivals and events are occasions to bring the community together and celebrate cultural bonding.

The atoll is also known for its natural beauty and unique environment. The lagoons, coral reefs and sandy beaches provide an idyllic backdrop for water sports, snorkeling, diving and relaxation. The underwater world of Addu City is rich in marine life and offers divers and snorkelers the opportunity to explore the fascinating underwater world.

In recent years, Addu City has undergone increasing development, including the expansion of infrastructure and tourism. Luxury resorts and accommodations have been created to provide visitors with a unique experience in this tranquil and secluded setting. However, despite modernization, Addu City has retained its cultural identity and charm, making it a popular destination for travelers who want to experience the authentic Maldivian lifestyle.

The history and culture of Addu City tell of a vibrant past and a dynamic present. As the second largest atoll in the Maldives, Addu City is not only a place of scenic beauty, but also a reflection of the diversity, history and way of life of Maldivian society. The people of Addu City proudly preserve their roots and welcome visitors to discover the beauty and spirit of the atoll.

From Gan to Hulhulé: Cities Through the Ages

The Maldives is known for its picturesque islands and stunning beaches, but it's also home to fascinating cities that have undergone amazing changes over time. Two such cities, Gan and Hulhulé, tell stories of change, development and adaptation that reflect the dynamism of the island nation.

Gan, located in the Addu Atoll, is a city that has a turbulent history behind it. During the British colonial period, Gan served as an important base for the British Air Force. The island was the scene of significant events during World War II and was later also a base during the Cold War. In the decades that followed, Gan underwent a gradual transformation from a military base to a thriving city. Infrastructure developed, and residents diversified their livelihoods from agriculture to the tourism industry. Today, Gan offers not only a rich history, but also a picturesque landscape lined with coconut palms that embodies the tranquility and charm of the Maldives. Hulhulé, an island in the North Malé Atoll, is another example of the transformation of Maldivian cities. This once small and nondescript island has become one of the most important hubs for international air travel. Malé International Airport, also known as Velana International Airport, is located on Hulhulé and plays a central role in connecting the Maldives to the rest of the world. The development of the airport has not only boosted tourism, but also boosted the country's trade and economy. Hulhulé is now a hub for travellers who want to experience the beauty of the Maldives, and at the same time a place that highlights the importance of international connection.

The transformation of Gan and Hulhulé is a reflection of the challenges and opportunities that the Maldives has experienced over time. The balance between preserving cultural identity, preserving nature and adapting to modern developments is a key issue for these cities and for the country as a whole. The people of Gan and Hulhulé have responded to these changes with determination and commitment, finding a unique balance between tradition and progress.

From the historic town of Gan to the changing island of Hulhulé, these cities represent the spirit of the Maldives: the ability to adapt while preserving cultural identity. They are a reflection of the journey the country has made to establish itself as a place of charm, beauty and dynamism. The stories of Gan and Hulhulé are stories of change, progress and pride in Maldivian identity.

Fuvahmulah: The unique island of the Maldives

Among the countless islands of the Maldives, Fuvahmulah stands out as a true gem of diversity and uniqueness. Located in the south of the country, Fuvahmulah is one of the few atoll islands that is not surrounded by a coral reef, but rather represents a single island with a stunning ecosystem. This peculiarity makes Fuvahmulah a true paradise for nature lovers, adventurers and explorers.

The geological formation of Fuvahmulah is fundamentally different from other islands in the Maldives. Instead of coral limestone, the island is made up of basaltic rock that was formed due to volcanic activity. This unique geological composition gives Fuvahmulah not only a unique landscape, but also a special biodiversity.

The lush vegetation on Fuvahmulah is impressive and different from the typical coral islands. Coconut palms, banana trees and lush green spaces characterize the image of the island. The fertile soil and abundant groundwater allow for the cultivation of fruits and vegetables, making Fuvahmulah a significant source of agricultural products in the Maldives.

The wildlife of Fuvahmulah is just as diverse. The island is a breeding ground for various species of birds, including those not found on other islands in the Maldives. The freshwater lakes and lagoons provide habitat for a variety of waterfowl and fish species. Fuvahmulah is also known for its population of reef sharks, which are native to the surrounding waters.

The people of Fuvahmulah have developed their own unique culture and dialect that is different from other regions of the Maldives. The island community has preserved its traditions, customs and way of life and brought them into harmony with the special environment of Fuvahmulah. Fishing plays an important role in people's livelihoods, as the waters around the island are rich in marine life.

The natural beauty of Fuvahmulah has attracted the attention of eco-tourists and nature lovers. The island offers opportunities for snorkeling, diving, hiking and bird watching. The marine life around Fuvahmulah is rich in coral formations, colorful fish species, and stunning marine life.

In recent years, Fuvahmulah has attracted an increasing number of visitors who want to experience the unique beauty and charm of the island. The government and community of Fuvahmulah are working to sustainably promote tourism while protecting the island's fragile environment.

Fuvahmulah is proof that there is far more to the Maldives than just white sandy beaches and turquoise waters. The island is a symbol of the diversity of nature and culture that can be found in this island nation. Fuvahmulah is a place where uniqueness can be experienced on every level, be it in the geological makeup, wildlife, vegetation or way of life of the people. It is an island that embodies the richness and beauty of the Maldives in all its facets.

Traditional handicrafts: handicrafts of the locals

Traditional craftsmanship in the Maldives is a living expression of the cultural identity and craftsmanship of the locals. Over generations, the people of the Maldives have developed various forms of craftsmanship that reflect their history, traditions and way of life. These works of art are not only aesthetically pleasing, but also a testament to the creative culture that thrives in this island nation.

A notable example of traditional craftsmanship in the Maldives is the production of 'Thundu Kunaa', traditional palm mats. These hand-woven mats are made from the leaves of the coconut palm and have a variety of uses in people's daily lives. From seating to sleeping mats, Thundu Kunaa are appreciated in many households and communities.

Another impressive craft is the production of 'hedika', the delicious sweet and savoury snacks made in Maldivian households. This culinary craft requires skill and tradition, as the preparation of Hedika is often passed down from generation to generation. These treats are not only a part of the local cuisine, but also an important part of celebrations and social gatherings.

The production of traditional boats, the "dhonis", is another outstanding art form in the Maldives. These handcrafted boats are made from coconut wood and coconut palm fibers and are vital for fishing and transportation. The technique of boat building is passed on to younger generations by skilled craftsmen to ensure that this important cultural heritage is preserved.

The art of "Koadi Beykalun", or wood carving, is also widespread in the Maldives. From ornate doors and shutters to decorative household items, the carved designs showcase the skills of craftsmen and the importance of ornamentation and detail in Maldivian culture.

The traditional craftsmanship of the Maldives is often shaped by deep values such as community, sustainability and cultural connectedness. Locals value the importance of their craft skills and cultural expressions and are committed to preserving these values for future generations.

The artisans of the Maldives are passionate about preserving the authenticity of their creations while facing the challenges of the modern world. Many artisans are looking for ways to showcase their products in the market and get fair value for their work. Craft skills are not only valued in communities, but also have the potential to contribute to the country's economy and tourism sector.

Overall, the traditional craftsmanship of the Maldives reflects not only the aesthetic beauty, but also the country's rich cultural depth and heritage. These art forms are a reflection of the identity, craftsmanship and sense of community of the locals, who pride themselves on maintaining their traditions while balancing them with the demands of the modern world.

Festivals and celebrations: cultural highlights throughout the year

The Maldives is known not only for its stunning beaches and dreamy resorts, but also for its diverse and vibrant festivals and celebrations that shape the cultural life of the locals. These events are highlights of the year and offer insights into the traditions, customs and sense of community in Maldivian society.

One of the most important religious festivals in the Maldives is Eid al-Fitr, the festival of breaking the fast at the end of the Muslim fasting month of Ramadan. It is a time of celebration, joy and gathering of families and friends. Locals dress in their best robes, visit the mosques for prayer, and share meals and gifts. The atmosphere during Eid al-Fitr is warm and festive, and there is a sense of unity and connectedness in the community.

Another significant religious festival is Eid al-Adha, the Feast of Sacrifice, which marks the conclusion of the pilgrimage to Mecca. During this festival, Muslims commemorate the willingness of Ibrahim (Abraham) to sacrifice his son in the name of God. Animal sacrifices are performed, and the meat is distributed among the needy. Eid al-Adha is a time of gratitude, prayer and social engagement, in which the community shows solidarity.

In addition to the religious festivals, there are also cultural celebrations that celebrate the heritage and traditions of the Maldives. The "Bodu Eid", the island festival, is an example of this. During this festival, people from different islands come together to enjoy cultural performances, traditional music, dancing and games. These events are opportunities to experience and celebrate the cultural diversity of the Maldives.

The National Day celebrations on July 26 are another important occasion in the Maldivian calendar. This day celebrates the country's independence from British rule in 1965. Parades, cultural performances, and events are held throughout the country to highlight pride in the Maldives' national identity and history.

The "Kuda Eid" or "Feeling Eid" is a lesser-known festival celebrated by the fishermen of the Maldives. This festival marks the end of the fishing season and is celebrated with traditions such as the "Bodu Beru" drum dance and festive meals. It is a time of recognition for those who work in the fishing industry, which is a significant part of Maldivian culture.

The festivals and celebrations of the Maldives are not only cultural events, but also opportunities to strengthen the sense of community, preserve traditions and celebrate the country's identity. They offer travelers and locals alike the opportunity to immerse themselves deeply in the culture and life of the Maldives and experience the warmth and hospitality of the locals. In a changing world, these festivals remain an important anchor for the preservation of Maldivian culture and its values.

Architecture of the Maldives: Traditional construction methods and modern trends

The architecture of the Maldives reflects the unique culture, environmental conditions, and needs of the locals. From traditional construction methods to modern trends, there is a fascinating variety of architectural styles that shape the appearance of the islands.

The traditional Maldivian architecture is closely linked to the conditions of the islands. Due to the limited availability of building materials and the need to adapt to tropical conditions, locals have developed unique construction methods over the centuries. The "bamboo verandas" are a characteristic feature of traditional houses. These verandas are made of bamboo logs and provide protection from the sun and rain. The houses are built on stilts to protect themselves from possible flooding.

The use of natural materials such as palm leaves, coconut wood and coral stones is another distinctive element of traditional architecture. The "bokkura", the traditional dwelling house, is often equipped with palm-thatched roofs and verandas. The "Bokkura" are not only functional but also aesthetically pleasing and fit perfectly into the natural environment of the Maldives.

However, with the modernization and influence of tourism, modern architectural trends have also established themselves in the Maldives. Luxurious resorts and hotels emerge with innovative design that combines the comfort of guests with the beauty of the surroundings. In many cases, care is taken to preserve the natural landscape and integrate it into the architectural concept.

An example of modern architecture is the famous overwater bungalows, which are often found in luxurious resorts. These bungalows stretch out over the clear waters, offering guests a unique way to enjoy the underwater world. The combination of modern comforts and eco-friendly design has helped make the Maldives a popular destination for discerning travelers.

The architecture of the Maldives faces the challenge of reconciling tradition and modernity. On the one hand, it is important to preserve the unique cultural identity and traditional building methods that make up the country's heritage. On the other hand, modern infrastructure and buildings must meet the needs of the growing population and tourism.

Overall, the architecture of the Maldives reflects the close relationship between humans and the environment. Adapting to natural conditions, using local materials and respecting the beauty of the islands are fundamental principles that characterize the country's architecture. Traditional construction methods and modern trends go hand in hand, helping to preserve the unique identity and beauty of the Maldives.

Bodu Beru: Maldivian Music and Dance

Music and dance play a central role in the cultural life of the Maldives, embodying the vibrant energy, joy and connectedness of the community. Among the many traditional forms of Maldivian music and dance, "Bodu Beru" occupies a prominent position. This captivating rhythm and dynamic movements are an essential part of Maldivian culture.

Bodu Beru is a traditional drum dance often performed at festive occasions, religious celebrations, and social gatherings. The main instruments are the "Bodu Beru" drums, which are made of wood and animal skin. The rhythm is created by a group of men playing the drums while others sing, clap and dance. The drums are often beaten in a repetitive sequence of beats, accompanied by energetic chants and expressive movements.

Bodu Beru's performances are infused with a lot of energy and passion. The rhythmic beats of the drums create a rousing atmosphere that inspires people to dance and sing along. The dancers move in circles, stamping their feet and moving their hands and hips to the beat of the music. The movements are often spontaneous and improvised, making each performance unique.

Bodu Beru is not only a form of entertainment, but also a way for people to express their joy, sense of community, and cultural identity. The songs and lyrics cover a variety of topics, from religious messages to stories from everyday life. They also serve as a means of social communication to spread news, share stories, and express emotions.

The significance of Bodu Beru extends far beyond cultural entertainment. It serves as a reminder of the roots and traditions of the Maldives, while also adapting to modern influences. In recent years, Bodu Beru has also gained international recognition and has become an important element of Maldivian tourism. Travelers will have the opportunity to attend demonstrations, experience the rich history and rhythmic beauty of this traditional art form.

Bodu Beru is a vibrant expression of the Maldives' creativity, community and cultural diversity. It connects people of all ages and backgrounds in a common rhythm and creates an atmosphere of joy and togetherness. In a changing world, Bodu Beru remains a symbol of the power of music to unite people and celebrate a country's cultural identity.

Trade and Souvenirs: Shopping in the Maldives

Shopping in the Maldives is a fascinating experience that offers travelers the opportunity to immerse themselves in the local culture and take a piece of the island nation home with them. The souvenirs, handicrafts, and products offered in the markets and shops of the Maldives reflect the country's diversity, craftsmanship and natural beauty.

One of the most popular souvenirs of the Maldives is the "Thundu Kunaa", traditional palm mats woven by hand. These mats are not only artfully crafted, but also practical and versatile. Often offered in a variety of sizes and patterns, they are an excellent way to take a piece of Maldivian culture home with you.

Another characteristic souvenir is products made from coconuts. From hand-carved coconut vessels to jewelry made from coconut shells, these products offer a glimpse into the creative use of natural resources. The locals are adept at carving coconuts into elaborate shapes and creating unique and authentic souvenirs.

Maldives Fish Market in Malé is a popular place to buy fresh fish and seafood. Here, visitors can get up close and personal with the rich fishing culture of the Maldives while choosing between the different types of fish, crabs, shrimp and other marine products. The market offers an insight into the local economy and the lifestyle of the locals.

In the souvenir shops of the resorts and towns, visitors can also find handmade jewelry, intricately designed textiles, traditional clothing, masks, paintings, and many other handicraft products. The variety of choices allows travelers to find unique and customized souvenirs that commemorate their trip and experiences in the Maldives.

A special highlight for shopping lovers are the "Thila" - the shops built on swimming platforms on the sea. Here, travelers can shop by the sea and purchase products such as jewelry, clothing, souvenirs, and handicrafts. This one-of-a-kind shopping experience combines the allure of shopping with the natural beauty of the Maldives.

It is important to note that many of the products in the Maldives are handmade and the locals are keen to promote traditional craftsmanship and local culture. By purchasing local products, visitors not only support the community, but also help preserve the cultural heritage of the Maldives.

Shopping in the Maldives is more than just acquiring goods; it's a way to immerse yourself in the stories, heritage, and passions of the locals. The souvenirs that can be found in the markets and shops tell of the rich culture and unique aesthetics of this fascinating island nation.

History of Tourism: The Evolution of Tourism

The history of tourism in the Maldives is a fascinating journey that has led from humble beginnings to one of the world's most popular tourist destinations. The development of tourism in the Maldives reflects not only the transformation of the global travel industry, but also the Maldives' efforts to share its unique natural beauty and culture.

The first tourists to visit the Maldives were adventurers and explorers attracted by the exoticism of the remote islands. During the 16th century, the Maldives was visited by Portuguese sailors who stopped on their voyages of discovery. Over time, a modest trade and exchange developed between the locals and the visitors, but tourism in the modern sense was not yet established.

It was in the 1970s that the Maldives opened its doors to international tourism, paving the way for the growth of the travel industry. Recognizing the potential of tourism as a source of economic income, the government began to take targeted measures to promote tourism. The development of resorts built directly on the islands was a milestone in this phase. These resorts offered guests the opportunity to experience the pristine beaches, crystal clear waters, and rich marine life of the Maldives.

Over time, the Maldives' efforts to establish itself as a dream destination for honeymoons and exclusive vacations have been rewarded. The unique beauty of the overwater bungalows that stretch across the azure waters and the luxurious amenities of the resorts attracted discerning travelers from all over the world. The Maldives became the epitome of paradisiacal relaxation, exotic luxury and romantic escapes.

However, the Maldives has not limited itself to the development of luxury resorts. In recent years, they have also increasingly promoted alternative forms of tourism, including ecotourism and sustainable tourism. The establishment of nature reserves, the protection of coral reefs and the promotion of environmentally friendly practices are important aspects to preserve the unique nature of the Maldives while supporting tourism.

Tourism in the Maldives has not only brought economic benefits, but has also fostered cultural diversity and exchange. Locals have the opportunity to work in the tourism industry, offer cultural activities and share their traditions with visitors.

The history of tourism in the Maldives is one of a continuous quest for a balance between economic growth and the protection of the country's unique environment and culture. In a changing world, tourism remains a key pillar of the Maldivian economy, carefully managed to preserve the islands' beauty and appeal for generations to come.

Paradisiacal Resorts: Luxury Accommodations in the Maldives

The Maldives is known worldwide for its stunning resorts that stretch like jewels across the clear, azure waters. These luxury accommodations offer visitors an unparalleled experience of beauty, relaxation and exclusive comfort amidst one of the most beautiful natural settings in the world.

The beginnings of resorts in the Maldives date back to the 1970s, when the government realized that tourism could become an important industry industry. The first resorts were built on some of the remote islands, offering visitors a unique way to experience the unspoiled beauty of the Maldives. These resorts were modest, but they laid the foundation for the growth of the luxury accommodations that adorn the islands today.

Over the years, resorts in the Maldives have become the epitome of luxury and sophistication. The overwater bungalows have become a hallmark of Maldivian resorts. These elegant and spacious villas span the crystal clear waters and offer stunning views of the ocean. Guests can dive into the water directly from their terraces to explore the impressive underwater world.

The resorts themselves are often ornately designed, offering a combination of modern design and traditional elements. Facilities range from exquisite restaurants serving international cuisine to luxurious spas offering a full range of wellness treatments. Activities such as snorkeling, diving, water sports, yoga and excursions in the surrounding area ensure that guests never get bored.

The service at the Maldivian resorts is known for its exceptional hospitality and attention to detail. Many resorts offer a personal butler service that takes care of guests' individual needs and ensures that every detail of their stay is perfect. The privacy and intimacy offered at these resorts make them a popular destination for honeymooners and romantic getaways.

The resorts in the Maldives are also pioneers in sustainable practices and environmental protection. Many resorts rely on eco-friendly technologies, renewable energy and the protection of the islands' fragile ecosystems.

This demonstrates the Maldives' commitment to providing its guests with not only luxurious experiences, but also sustainable and respectful interaction with nature.

The paradisiacal resorts of the Maldives are far more than just accommodations; they are oases of relaxation, enjoyment and beauty. They offer guests the opportunity to immerse themselves in a world of unsurpassed luxury while admiring the natural splendor of the Maldives. Each resort has its own unique atmosphere, but they all share a common aspiration to provide visitors with an exceptional experience amidst the picturesque backdrop of the Indian Ocean.

Dreamy beaches and crystal clear waters: the attractions of the islands

The Maldives is undoubtedly known for its stunning beaches and crystal clear turquoise waters. These natural attractions form the heart of the Maldivian paradise and are a magnet for travelers from all over the world.

The beaches of the Maldives are like something out of a dream. The fine, white grain of sand shimmers in the sunlight and stretches along the coastlines in a seemingly endless expanse. The beaches are not only picturesque, but also incredibly relaxing. The gentle waves of the Indian Ocean lap the coasts, inviting visitors to bathe, swim and relax.

What makes the beaches of the Maldives so special is their privacy. Many resorts have their own private beaches that are only accessible to guests. This means that travelers have the freedom to enjoy the pristine beauty of the islands at their leisure. The beaches are the perfect place to admire sunrises and sunsets, take romantic walks or just relax in a hammock.

The crystal clear waters of the Maldives are another highlight that captivates visitors. Visibility underwater can often be as high as 30 meters, making the Maldives one of the best snorkeling and diving destinations in the world. The colorful marine life is rich with coral reefs, colorful fish, sea turtles, manta rays, and a variety of marine life.

The lagoons of the Maldives are a sanctuary for marine fauna and flora, offering guests the opportunity to experience the beauty of the oceans up close. Many resorts offer snorkeling and diving trips that allow visitors to explore the fascinating underwater world. Swimming with whale sharks and manta rays is an unforgettable experience that visitors often consider the highlight of their stay.

However, the attractions of the Maldivian islands go far beyond the beaches and water. The islands also offer ample opportunity for activities such as water sports, kayaking, stand-up paddleboarding, parasailing and fishing. Excursions to the nearby islands and atolls allow visitors to learn about the local culture, local life, and traditional handicrafts.

The Maldives is a place where nature can be experienced in all its glory and perfection. The picturesque beaches, clear waters and diverse marine life create an environment that combines relaxation, adventure and unforgettable experiences. The attractions of the Maldivian islands are not only visual spectacles, but also an invitation to indulge the senses and enjoy the beauty of nature to the fullest.

Water Sports Paradise: Activities for the Adventurous

The Maldives is not only a place of relaxation and rejuvenation, but also a true paradise for adventurous travelers looking for exciting water sports. With their clear waters, warm temperatures and diverse underwater landscapes, the Maldivian islands offer a wide range of activities that will get the pulse of adventure lovers racing.

Diving is undoubtedly one of the most popular water sports in the Maldives. The surrounding coral reefs are home to an amazing variety of marine life, including colorful corals, tropical fish, turtles, rays, and even majestic sharks. The visibility underwater is often impressive, making diving an unforgettable experience. Diving schools and resorts offer courses for beginners to advanced divers who want to explore the underwater world in all its glory.

For those who want to explore the underwater world without diving equipment, snorkeling is the perfect choice. The shallow lagoons and clear waters of the Maldives offer ideal conditions for snorkeling adventures. Snorkelers can explore colorful coral reefs, see fish in all the colors of the rainbow, and get up close and personal with the beauty of the underwater world.

For adrenaline junkies, there are also opportunities for water sports such as jet skiing, parasailing, kitesurfing and windsurfing in the Maldives. The warm winds and calm waters of the lagoons create optimal conditions for these activities. Water sports centers at the resorts provide professional equipment and guidance to ensure guests can enjoy their adventures to the fullest.

For those who prefer a slower pace, kayaking and stand-up paddling are a great way to explore the islands' shorelines. These activities are not only fun, but also an excellent way to explore the surroundings at your leisure and admire the beauty of nature.

The Maldives is also an excellent destination for deep-sea anglers looking for exciting fishing experiences. The waters around the islands are rich in fish stocks such as tuna, mahi-mahi, wahoo and marlin. Fishing trips are offered by experienced fishermen and charter companies who show guests the best spots and techniques.

Whether you're an experienced water sports enthusiast or looking to immerse yourself in this exciting world for the first time, the Maldives offers a wealth of activities to appeal to both adventure seekers and nature lovers. The combination of adrenaline and the natural beauty of the islands makes these activities unforgettable experiences that travelers will remember long after they return.

Maldivian Art Scene: Modern Artists and Their Works

At first glance, the Maldivian art scene may seem overshadowed by the stunning natural scenery, but it is vibrant and diverse. In recent years, a growing community of artists has developed in the Maldives, using their talents to capture the culture and beauty of the islands in creative ways.

Modern Maldivian art is characterized by a mixture of tradition and innovation. Many artists draw inspiration from the colors, shapes, and motifs of local culture, creating works that reflect the islands' rich history and natural splendor. At the same time, they are looking for new forms of expression and experimentation to bring in contemporary themes and ideas.

A significant feature of the Maldivian art scene is the use of various mediums and techniques. Painting, sculpture, photography, digital art and installations all find a place in the artists' works. This diversity reflects the different perspectives and expressions that the artists bring to their works.

Some Maldivian artists have managed to gain international recognition. Her works have been exhibited in galleries around the world and have attracted the attention of art lovers and collectors. These artists help bring the Maldivian art scene to the global stage and strengthen the cultural identity of the islands.

The themes covered in the works of modern Maldivian artists are varied. From addressing environmental issues and sustainability to exploring identity and social issues, artists use their art to express their thoughts and feelings and create awareness of current issues.

The art galleries in the Maldives offer artists the opportunity to showcase their works to the public. In these galleries, visitors can gain insight into the creative diversity of the islands and purchase local artwork that reminds them of their time in paradise.

The Maldivian art scene may still be growing, but it has already undergone an impressive evolution. The artists in the Maldives help to preserve and develop the culture and identity of the islands in a creative way. Their works are not only an expression of their individual creativity, but also a reflection of the rich beauty and depth of Maldivian culture.

Environmental Protection and Sustainability: The Maldives' Efforts

The Maldives is known not only for its breathtaking beauty, but also for its commitment to environmental protection and sustainability. In the face of threats from climate change, rising sea levels and ocean pollution, the Maldivian authorities and the community have made significant efforts to protect the islands' unique environment.

One of the most important issues facing the Maldives is climate change and the associated sea level rise. Due to their low geographical altitude, the islands are particularly vulnerable to the effects of climate change. The government of the Maldives has therefore placed a focus on climate protection measures and has made international efforts to reduce greenhouse gas emissions.

A notable project of the Maldives is the transition to renewable energy. Many resorts and communities are turning to solar energy to meet their energy needs and reduce their environmental footprint. This not only helps mitigate climate change, but also reduces dependence on fossil fuels.

Another focus of environmental protection measures in the Maldives is the protection of the marine environment. The underwater world of the islands is a valuable ecosystem that must be preserved. Coral reefs, which are home to numerous species, are at the heart of this effort. Marine sanctuaries have been established to preserve the reefs and curb overfishing.

Plastic waste is a global environmental crisis that also affects the Maldives. To counteract this, the Maldivian authorities have taken measures to reduce the use of single-use plastic. Some resorts have completely banned plastic packaging and are focusing on environmentally friendly alternatives.

The Maldives also embraces sustainable tourism as part of its environmental protection strategy. Resorts pursue eco-friendly practices such as water and energy conservation, waste management, and the protection of local wildlife. Guests are often encouraged to be environmentally conscious and participate in efforts to protect the islands.

In addition to these measures, education and awareness-raising play an important role. The Maldivian government and non-profit organizations run programs to educate the population about environmental issues and make them aware of the importance of protecting the environment.

The Maldives' efforts in the field of environmental protection and sustainability are inspiring and show that even in a country blessed by natural wonders, serious efforts are needed to protect the environment. The Maldives is setting an example for the rest of the world on how a conscious approach to nature and sustainable practices can help preserve the beauty of the islands for generations to come.

Travel Tips: Practical Information for Visiting the Maldives

Visiting the Maldives is undoubtedly a dream of many travelers who want to experience the breathtaking beauty of the islands. To make your stay go smoothly and help you get the most out of your trip, here are some practical information and tips that can help you plan and execute your trip.

1. **When to go:** The Maldives is a year-round destination as the climate is always warm and tropical. However, the best time to visit depends on your interests. The dry season from November to April is popular for diving and water sports, while the low season from May to October ensures cheaper prices.
2. **Visa:** Upon entry, most tourists receive a free 30-day visa. You will need a valid passport that is valid for at least six months.
3. **Health:** No special vaccinations are required to enter the Maldives. Nevertheless, it is advisable to keep

the standard vaccinations up to date and to inform yourself about any health risks.
4. **Currency:** The currency of the Maldives is the Maldivian Rufiyaa (MVR). Most resorts and tourist resorts also accept U.S. dollars and euros. Credit cards are widely accepted.
5. **Language:** The official language is Dhivehi, but English is used as a lingua franca in many tourist areas.
6. **Clothing:** Since the Maldives is a Muslim country, it is appropriate to dress respectfully in public. Casual clothing is acceptable in the resorts, but in urban areas and on inhabited islands, it is advisable to wear shoulder- and knee-covering clothing.
7. **Communications:** Most resorts offer Wi-Fi, but reception on remote islands can be limited. It is advisable to buy a local SIM card if you want to stay in touch.
8. **Gratuities:** Tipping is often included at the resorts, but it is customary to give extra tips to the staff if the service was satisfactory.
9. **Reservations:** If you are planning a visit to one of the luxury resorts, it is advisable to book in advance as they are often fully booked.

10. **Environmental protection:** The Maldives attaches great importance to the protection of its environment. Respect nature and marine life, and avoid collecting coral or feeding fish.
11. **Baggage:** Check your airline's baggage policy, as there may be restrictions on the weight and size of your baggage.
12. **Airport Transfers:** Most resorts offer transfers from Malé International Airport to the islands. These transfers can be by boat or seaplane, depending on the distance.

By following this practical information and tips, you can ensure that your trip to the Maldives is memorable and enjoyable. Remember to do your research before your trip to respect the local culture and the conditions on the islands. Enjoy the paradisiacal beauty of the Maldives to the fullest!

Dive into History: Archaeological Sites and Wrecks

The underwater world of the Maldives is not only home to rich marine biodiversity, but also fascinating insights into the history of the islands. Archaeological sites and sunken wrecks tell stories of times gone by and offer divers the opportunity to immerse themselves in history.

Many of the archaeological sites in the Maldives date back to the time of the Buddhist kingdom that existed on the islands before the arrival of Islam. These sites often consist of remains of temples, monasteries, and other structures that once reflected the religious and cultural life of society at the time. Divers can discover ancient stone statues, inscriptions, and artifacts that document the history of that era.

Particularly noteworthy is the dive site on Thoddoo, where an ancient Buddhist temple complex lies underwater. The remains of this site offer fascinating glimpses into the religious life of the people who once lived in the Maldives.

In addition to the archaeological sites, sunken wrecks are also an exciting destination for divers interested in history. The Maldives is located on ancient trade routes that were used by ships from all over the world. Over the centuries, some of these ships have sunk, leaving wrecks on the seabed.

A well-known wreck is the "Maldives Victory" wreck, a cargo ship that sank near Malé in 1981. The wreck not only offers an impressive underwater spectacle, but also a reminder of the recent maritime history of the Maldives.

Diving at archaeological sites and wrecks often requires a certain amount of experience and caution. It is important to follow the rules and guidelines for the protection of these historic sites in order to preserve their integrity. Divers should also check the local regulations and conditions before embarking on such adventures.

The opportunity to immerse yourself in the history of the Maldives while exploring the fascinating underwater world makes diving in archaeological sites and wrecks a unique experience for history buffs and diving enthusiasts alike.

Maldivian Literature: Writers and Their Works

Maldivian literature has a rich history that spans centuries and includes a mix of oral traditions, written art, and modern creativity. Although Maldivian literature is often less well-known than the literary traditions of other cultures, it still has a deep significance for the identity and cultural richness of the islands.

The oldest records of Maldivian literature are written in Dhivehi, the language of the Maldives. The stories have traditionally been passed down orally and include myths, legends and folk tales that reflect the culture and history of the islands. These oral traditions are a precious treasure that has been passed down from generation to generation.

The arrival of Islam in the Maldives in the 12th century brought with it Arabic scriptures and Islamic literature. These influences are reflected in the writings of Maldivian scholars and poets who wrote religious poems and works to strengthen the Muslim identity and spirituality of the islands.

Over time, Maldivian literature continued to evolve and absorb modern influences. In the

20th century, writers began to publish poems, short stories, and novels in Dhivehi. An important writer of this period was Abdul Sattar, who addressed the social and political issues of the Maldives through his poetry and prose.

With the introduction of printing technologies in the 20th century, the publication and distribution of literature was facilitated. Modern Maldivian writers such as Ahmed Shafeeq, Mohamed Jameel Didi and Abdulla Sadiq tackled a wide range of themes in their works, from social issues to love and identity.

The Maldivian literary landscape has also evolved into the contemporary era, with young writers publishing poems and stories in a variety of media, including books, magazines, and online platforms. This allows for a wider dissemination of Maldivian literature and contributes to the cultural diversity of the islands.

The stories, poems and writings of Maldivian literature are a reflection of the islands' diverse history, culture and identity. They tell of the dreams, hopes and challenges of the Maldivian people and help to reflect the unique voice and creativity of the Maldives in the literary world.

Clash of Cultures: Maldives and the Influence of Tourism

The Maldives is known not only for its stunning beaches and clear waters, but also for the rich cultural diversity that exists on the islands. The clash of cultures in the Maldives reflects the islands' long history as a hub on Indian Ocean trade routes. With the arrival of tourism in recent decades, the cultural landscape of the Maldives has evolved and changed.

Maldivian culture is a mix of different influences, including Arabic, Indian, African, and Southeast Asian elements. This cultural diversity is the result of centuries of trade and exchange with different civilizations. The clash of cultures is evident in the language, architecture, cuisine and traditions of the Maldives.

With the advent of tourism in the 1970s, the Maldives began to experience a new phase of cultural interaction. The opening of resorts and the influx of tourists from all over the world brought new ideas, perspectives and lifestyles to the islands. The locals had the opportunity to connect with people from different countries and share their culture.

Tourism also brought changes in the economic structure of the Maldives. Traditionally, fishing has been the most important industry, but tourism quickly became a driving force. The locals started working in the tourism sector, which led to a cultural exchange between the guests and the locals.

The clash of cultures also manifested itself in the culinary scene of the Maldives. Resorts offer not only local Maldivian dishes, but also international cuisine to cater to the different tastes of guests. This culinary diversity reflects the Maldives' openness to new influences and adds to its cultural dynamism.

Despite the positive aspects, tourism has also brought challenges. Cultural adaptation to the needs and expectations of tourists has sometimes led to tensions. Locals work hard to preserve their identity while reaping the benefits of tourism.

Overall, tourism has enriched and expanded the encounter of cultures in the Maldives. The islands have managed to preserve their unique identity while benefiting from the positive aspects of cultural exchange. The cultural diversity of the Maldives will continue to play an important role as the islands continue to develop and stay in touch with the global community.

Looking to the Future: The Challenges and Opportunities for the Maldives

The Maldives faces a myriad of challenges and opportunities as it moves towards an uncertain future. Despite their breathtaking beauty and tourism potential, the islands face a number of environmental, economic and social challenges that require careful consideration and action.

One of the biggest challenges facing the Maldives is undoubtedly climate change. As a flat country with low elevation above sea level, the Maldives is particularly vulnerable to sea level rise and more extreme weather events. The government and the population have recognized that climate change is an existential threat and are working hard to develop adaptation strategies to minimize its impacts.

Another problem is pollution, especially related to plastics and waste. Tourism brings with it an increased amount of waste, which puts a strain on the islands' limited resources.

Efforts to promote environmental awareness and recycling are underway to reduce the impact of waste on nature.

Economic diversification is another challenge. The Maldives is heavily dependent on the tourism sector, which makes it vulnerable to economic fluctuations and external shocks. There is a growing need to promote other sectors of the economy in order to reduce dependence on tourism and strengthen resilience to economic changes.

Despite these challenges, the Maldives also offers a variety of opportunities. The rich marine biodiversity and breathtaking beauty of the islands make them a paradise for nature and adventure lovers. Sustainable tourism and the protection of the environment could contribute to sustainable economic development while preserving the unique nature of the Maldives.

The promotion of education and technological innovation also offers opportunities. The younger generation of Maldives has access to education and technology, which gives them the opportunity to grow in various fields and contribute to the development of the islands.

International cooperation is crucial to address the challenges and seize the opportunities. The Maldives is part of the global community and works with international organizations and countries to find common solutions to climate change, environmental protection and economic diversification.

The outlook for the future of the Maldives is complex and multifaceted. The islands face challenges that are not easy to overcome, but they also have the opportunity to protect and develop their unique nature and culture. Through careful planning, sustainable practices, and an engaged population, the Maldives can shape its future and respond to the opportunities that present themselves.

Epilogue

This concludes our fascinating journey through the Maldives, a country of unparalleled beauty, rich culture and impressive history. From crystal clear waters to stunning coral reefs, from vibrant cities to secluded islands, the Maldives has taken us to the depths of its diversity and splendor.

As we close the pages of this book, the realization remains that the Maldives is more than just a tropical paradise. They are a place of historical importance, cultural diversity and ecological richness. Developments over the centuries have shaped a nation that is proud of its past and optimistic about the future.

We had the opportunity to explore the history of the Maldives – from early settlements to modern independence. We discovered the diverse culture, religious influences, art scene and maritime lifestyle of the islands. We looked at the challenges and opportunities facing the Maldives, especially in terms of environmental protection, sustainability and the tourism sector.

The Maldives is at a turning point in its history as it faces the global challenges of climate change, sustainability and economic development. It is a time of rethinking, innovation and commitment to preserve the unique beauty and culture of the islands while creating a sustainable future.

We hope this book has given you an in-depth look at the Maldives – whether as a travel guide, a source of inspiration, or a way to learn more about this fascinating nation. The Maldives will continue to charm and attract people from all over the world, and we are grateful to have been able to share a glimpse of this magical country.

With these thoughts, we conclude our journey through the Maldives. May the beauty and diversity of the islands live on in our hearts as we embark on our own journeys and discoveries.

Printed in Great Britain
by Amazon